I0440775

This book is dedicated to my first born son, Andrew Jacob. I am so proud of my Olympic athlete and bio-engineer.

# A Close Up Look at

# Bryce Canyon National

# Park

## By Josie Zayac

Bryce Canyon is the place

where rocks form hoodoos.

Who wants to go?

I hope that you do!

Take a close look.

What do you see?

I see a huge rock that is sedimentary.

Rocks formed from other rocks, how elementary!

Take a close look.

What do you see?

I see the branches of a gnarly tree.

Take a close look.
What do you see?

A trumpet-shaped flower,
called a stoneseed.

Take a close look.
What do you see?

It's called a
paintbrush,
the bristles
I see.

# Take a close look.
# What do you see?

The fur of a mule deer
mother and baby.

Take a close look.

What do you see?

# A bristlecone pine
# as old as can be.

*This tree is 1,600 years old!*

Take a close look.

What do you see?

A window in the
rocks,
through it I see.

Take a close look.
What do you see?

It looks like ice cream, I hope it's for me!

Take a close look.
What do you see?

It's a sego lily,
as pretty as can be.

Take a close look.
What do you see?

The wind is so strong, it twisted this tree.

Take a close look.
What do you see?
The leaves of an aspen,
it's a type of tree.

Take a close look.
What do you see?

So many wildflowers,
a beautiful sight to see.

Take a close look.

What do you see?

There are so many beautiful

sights, you'd agree.

Go out into nature
and look all around.
So many treasures
beg to be found.

# Facts about Bryce Canyon National Park, Utah

- Officially established in 1928
- Best known for the hoodoos, misshapen rocks formed by erosion
- Highest point is 9,115 feet
- Named after Ebenezer and Mary Bryce who lived there from 1875-1880
- Pinyon and juniper trees grow at low elevations
- Fir, aspen, bristlecone pines and ponderosa pines grow at various elevations

# Look for other National Park books by Dr. Josie Zayac

- A Close Up Look at Bryce Canyon National Park
- A Close Up Look at Crater Lake National Park
- A Close Up Look at Cuyahoga Valley National Park
- A Close Up Look at Joshua Tree National Park
- A Close Up Look at Redwood National and State Parks
- A Close Up Look at Rocky Mountain National Park
- A Close Up Look at Sequoia National Park
- A Close Up Look at Theodore Roosevelt National Park
- A Close Up Look at Zion National Park

www.ingramcontent.com/pod-product-compliance
Lightning Source LLC
Chambersburg PA
CBHW050929290526
45792CB00002B/949